2005 PRESIDENTIAL ADDRESS

"Cross Border Ticket Influence"

given by

John King

Presented at the Friends Meeting House,
Mount Street, Manchester on 4th March 2006
And repeated at the Southwick Community Centre,
Southwick, West Sussex on 18th March 2006

The Transport Ticket Society
2009

Comments etc. regarding this publication are welcome;
please write to the Hon. Secretary,

Alan Peachey
4 The Sycamores,
BISHOPS STORTFORD.
CM23 5JR

The production of this publication has been made possible thanks
to the bequest to the Society by the late Robin Pallett
who was a member for about 40 years

Further copies of this and other Publications may be obtained from the
Society's Publication Sales Officer:

Steve Skeavington
6 Breckbank,
Forest Town,
MANSFIELD.
NG19 0PZ

ISBN 978-0-903209-64-9

Published by
The Transport Ticket Society
4 The Sycamores, Bishops Stortford. CM23 5JR.

Printed by
DOPPLER PRESS
5 Wates Way, Brentwood, Essex. CM15 9TB

This is a subject which has interested me for many years, and which from time to time has featured in Journal in one form or another. However, it is one of those subjects which have no defined boundaries, and the examples which are illustrated are far from being exhaustive. On the contrary, there will inevitably be other, equally valid, examples which have not occurred to me, or are unknown to me. I very much hope that this address will stimulate discussion and additional contributions.

The subject, "Cross Border Ticket Influence" is a truly inter-modal one, and I have attempted to include examples from all forms of transport – so that hopefully there will be something of interest to everyone. The water transport content is rather thin, principally because my knowledge in this area is likewise. I have to confess, also, to a bias towards pre-printed tickets, and so I shall not stray too far into the realms of modern machines and machine issues, where my knowledge as well as my enthusiasm, is limited. To conclude these introductory comments, perhaps I might add that, whilst most of the tickets illustrated are my own, several are the property of other members, and I should like to particularly acknowledge the assistance of Gordon Fairchild and Michael Stewart in providing the relevant illustrations. I am also deeply indebted to David Harman for his expertise in putting the presentation together.

It seems logical to start with the invention which can justifiably claim to have transcended most geographical boundaries, namely the Edmondson card. Most countries which have had railways within their borders have at some stage used Edmondson card tickets, and it is the few exceptions (such as Malta) which are noteworthy. This gives me a somewhat spurious reason for illustrating a handful of examples from countries which are not well-known as Edmondson users – Jamaica (often erroneously quoted as "one which didn't"), Barbados and the Philippines (1).

(1)

Sticking with Edmondsons for the time being, we can consider individual styles which have crossed borders by virtue of colonial connections. It is not easy to identify early British styles which have been directly adopted overseas, but it does appear that the initial simplicity of the British Edmondson (often not even being titled) was transported to early colonial undertakings. Here are three very plain tickets from England (all pre-1880) (2).

(2)

 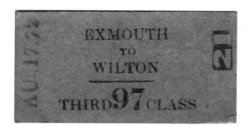

1

and others from various different territories – firstly from pre-Union South Africa, where the earliest of the three tickets (016) from the Cape Government Railway (although untitled) is ironically the one which displays the most conditions. The other two require little explanation, as they are both clearly titled (3).

(3)

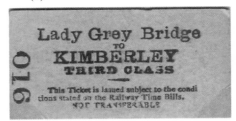  

Then there are three from India – an untitled issue (873) from the Madras Railway dated 1893, a similarly plain example from the Great Indian Peninsular Railway (363), which does in fact have the company's initials on the back, and a very rare issue from the Kokilamukh State Railway, in the tea-growing area of Assam, dated 1895 (4).

(4)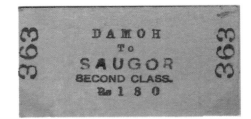

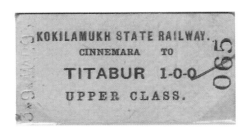

Finally there are examples from the Mauritius Railway (dated 1878) and the Imperial Railways of North China (dated 1906), which are of remarkably similar appearance (5).

(5)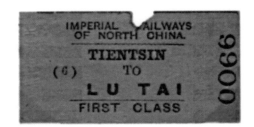

Leaving British connections, we can immediately see that pre-1918 German tickets from South West Africa (now Namibia) and Tanganyika, are of unmistakable German origin and format (6).

(6)

We can see the same direct connection between tickets of Portugal and Angola (7),

(7)

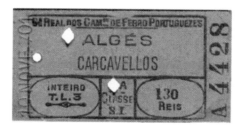 

Italy and Libya (8),

(8)

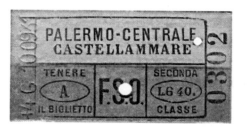 

France and French West Africa (Senegal) (9).

(9)

What is at least as interesting here is what is missing – it seems a certainty that there will have been German-printed tickets in both Kamerun (Cameroon) and Togoland (Togo) prior to the redistribution of those territories to other powers after the First World War, but I have never seen examples. Likewise, the railway built by the Italians in Somaliland will have had tickets – probably in recognisable Italian format – but again these have never come to light to my knowledge.

A rather less obvious connection is illustrated by the next two tickets – the first being a standard Belgian issue from the Chemin de Fer Vicinal, and the other being from the Egyptian Delta Light Railways (10). This seems to reflect the early activities in Egypt on the part of Edouard Louis Joseph, Baron Empain, who was involved with the construction of railways and tramways in the late 19th. Century in his native Belgium, as well as various other territories, and who arrived in Egypt in January 1904. In the event his ambitions for railway construction there were to some extent thwarted by the loss of key contracts to British companies, so the ticket illustrated was probably short-lived.

(10)

Next we have a scarce 1902 Edmondson from Puerto Rico (11). When I came across this in my collection in the course of preparing this talk, I identified it as being in Italian style, but another member was adamant that it displayed Portuguese influence. On the other hand, it is not dissimilar to one or two early Spanish tickets which I have seen…….So here are examples of all three possible influences, all dated between 1892 and 1920, by way of comparison. Spain would perhaps be the most logical connection with Spanish-speaking Puerto Rico, but I still feel personally that the Italian style has the edge.

(11)

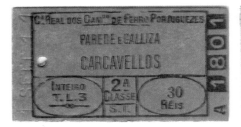  

An interesting example of cross-border ticket production is provided by Tanganyika Railways, during its British (as opposed to German) colonial days. For some years T.R. tickets were printed in India (it is believed by the North Western Railway there), and they display a very Indian feature, namely quoting the initials of the issuing railway on the back (12).

(12).

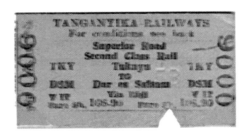 

This feature has also been noted on tickets of the Aden Railway (or at least the very small number which have come to light) (13), and also on the basis of a couple of tickets which I have seen for sale on a well-known on-line auction site but didn't secure myself, Mesopotomian Railways. (Interestingly, "M.R" is also known on the tickets of a genuinely Indian operation, the Morvi Railway).

(13)

We seem to be spending quite a lot of time on African railways in this talk so far, but for those whose interests lie in quite different areas there will be other items of interest before too long. However, we must firstly take a look at Rhodesia, for a number of worthwhile items come from those parts. Firstly, we have a ticket titled Chemins de Fer du Katanga" from Elisabethville (in the Belgian Congo – subsequently Zaire, and now the Democratic Republic of Congo) to Ndola, which seems to have been produced by the Beira and Mashonaland Railway, i.e. the railway of destination rather than origin (14).

(14)

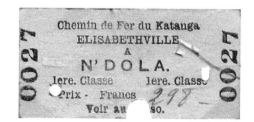 

Presumably there was some revenue-sharing reason for this approach (which is not unknown in the context of some U.K. tram/bus joint operations), but it is certainly unusual on international rail tickets. Rhodesia was subsequently administered by Britain as two separate territories – Northern and Southern Rhodesia. In 1964 Northern Rhodesia was granted independence and became Zambia, while in 1965 (Southern) Rhodesia made a Unilateral Declaration of Independence, and was ostracised by most of its neighbours, as well as the rest of the world. These events had interesting effects on the tickets of what had become Zambian Railways. Prior to Zambian independence, Rhodesian tickets had all been in the same long-standing style, and initially Zambian Railways appear to have continued to have their tickets printed in Rhodesia (I do not know the location of the printing works, but it is a reasonable bet that it was in Salisbury (now Harare). This situation appears not to have lasted for very long, and by 1970 ZR Edmondsons were in a different format, which was clearly borrowed from East African Railways and Harbours (or successors). We can only speculate as to whether Zambian Railways made the change to avoid dealing with Ian Smith's UDI regime, or whether Rhodesian Railways decided to cancel the contract themselves, for whatever reasons. As it transpired, Zambia did not use Edmondsons for very long in any event – but nevertheless there was time for a third, possibly domestically produced type; none of these are particularly common, and I would regard the Rhodesian-produced ones as scarce (15, 16).

(15)

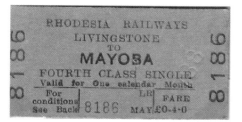 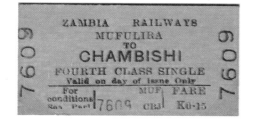

(16)

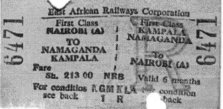 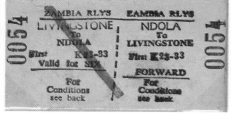 

Well into the 1960s, there were through services from Rhodesia to Mozambique, and this produced some interesting tickets for our consideration. Here are three, all clearly Rhodesian prints: a Rhodesia Railways titled ticket for a journey to Beira entirely within Mozambique, and in Portuguese, and a Beira Railway titled one for the reverse journey, plus a Beira Railway titled issue from Beira to Blantyre, the then capital of Nyasaland (now Malawi) (17).

(17)

Before leaving this part of Africa, we should perhaps move southwards and take a look at the rather odd situation which applied in Bechuanaland (which had the status of a British protectorate until it became independent as Botswana in 1966). This is a large territory, but a very large part of it is desert, and there is effectively only one thoroughfare, for road and rail, on its easternmost edge. The railway in question joins South Africa to what was originally Rhodesia, and prior to independence was operated by Rhodesia Railways.

Until independence, and indeed for 10 years afterwards, Bechuanaland used the currency of South Africa – pounds sterling until 1961, and Rands thereafter. The railway's tickets were printed by either South African Railways or Rhodesia Railways – I have been unable to determine the basis for which was involved with any particular issue.   Unfortunately I have been unable to locate any examples prior to 1960, but here we have a number of different 4th. Class singles; the first, for a short local journey into Gaberones, the state capital, is printed by S.A.R with fare in sterling and specifies "R.R Single" (1060), another "Batch Rate" issue from Palapye in Bechuanaland to Braamfontein in South Africa again has a sterling fare but is printed by R.R (0091), an S.A.R print between the Bechuanaland towns of Gaberones and Francistown, but with fare in Rands (5809), and similar between Palapye and Francistown but printed by R.R (7699). Finally, there is a 2nd. Class issue again printed by R.R, which shows the fare in Pula, Botswana's own currency which was introduced in 1976 (3983) (18, 19).

(18)

(19)

The feature whereby tickets are printed by an authority in a currency foreign to it is by no means unique to Botswana. On the contrary, there are a number of examples which come to mind; here are one or two – the Swiss postbuses operate certain routes into and through non-Swiss territory, so tickets in both Austrian schillings and Italian lire are known (20),

(20)

and Keretapi Tanah Melayu (formerly the Malayan Railway) has a terminus in another sovereign state with a different currency, namely Singapore (21).

(21)

Finally in this section, we should not overlook cross-border ticket influence which arose as a result of war. In European territories annexed by Germany during the Second World War, there are several examples of German-printed tickets which are distinctive in terms of the journeys which they represent and sometimes the language of the territory. Firstly, there are three tickets from Latvia, including a monthly card, all obviously German prints, and showing fares in Reichsmarks (22).

(22)

In contrast, neighbouring Lithuania seems to have retained its own ticket format during the period of the occupation – here are examples of pre-war and wartime issues (the latter with Reichsmark fare) (23).

(23)

Austria (technically an annexation, rather than an occupation) also seems to have retained its long-standing ticket designs during the occupation - these will be familiar to many members, and are illustrated here by three tickets, the middle of which again has a Reichsmark fare, and the right-hand one is an entirely standard post-war issue, but from the only station on Liechtenstein soil, Schaan-Vaduz (24).

(24)

Germany adopted a standard pattern for their platform tickets before the war, with blue bands at either end, and again these are fairly well-known to collectors. Here is an early post-war example, with price in Deutschmarks, together with a wartime issue from Austria (Wien Südbahnhof), priced in Reichsmarks, and one from Czechoslovakia priced in Krone. The last of these is particularly interesting in that it is bilingual – German language on the front, and Czech on the back (25,26).

(25)

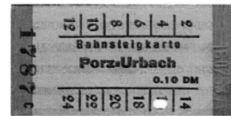  

(26)

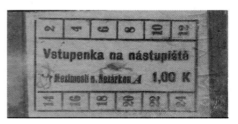

It would be good to be able to report that there are overseas platform tickets known which were based on the design of those issued by one or more British railway companies; unfortunately, I cannot claim this with any confidence. However, there is a clear acknowledgment on the part of a number of railway companies that platform tickets should be sufficiently different in appearance from travel tickets, for ease of examination by station barrier staff. Thus the concept of a distinctive overprint has been adopted by companies across the world – in the U.K. we are most familiar with red blobs and red and green diamonds, among others, but different symbols have been used elsewhere for the same purpose. Here we can see a couple of choice U.K. examples (27),

(27)

together with others from France, Hong Kong and Iraq (28).

(28)

Before leaving the Edmondson, here is a rather unusual item from the Great Western Railway. I am not sure that it really comes under the heading of cross-border influence, but it is worth seeing, and I am indebted to Gordon Fairchild for bringing it to my attention (29).

(29)

We now need to move on to that other great British invention (in ticket terms at least), the punch-type. It would be fair to say that this did not achieve the near-universal penetration already noted in relation to the Edmondson (certainly its use in non-British territories was sporadic), but nevertheless punch-types have been used in diverse territories (some, as we will see, rather surprising ones).

Two of the earliest printers of punch tickets were T.J. Whiting and Bell Punch, and they appear to have competed for the business of supplying tickets, punches and other equipment to the tramway and horse-bus companies which were established during the 1880s and 1890s – primarily U.K. operators, but there is clear evidence from early Whiting catalogues that their business extended well beyond these shores from fairly early days. Here, in order to illustrate the Whiting style, and in particular their distinctive serial numbers, are tickets from the Southampton Tramways Co, the Hull Street Tramways Co, and the South London Tramways Co (30).

(30)

The last of these is the earliest of the three, and is in Whiting's earlier "wide" format. From overseas we have the East India Tramways Co. Ltd (Karachi) and the Rangoon Steam Tramway Co. Ltd. (31). All of these have the distinctive Whiting serial numbers which, in the absence of an imprint, is in most cases the sole identifying feature of Whiting tickets.

(31)

 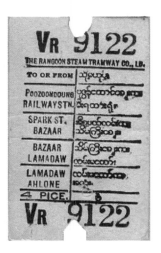

Perhaps more surprising than the Karachi and Rangoon examples, bearing in mind that both were colonial operations at the time, Whiting also claimed several French Tramway companies as customers in their catalogues. An early example from the Tramways de Calais can be found in Wiener's "Passenger Tickets", and a slightly later one with sub-heading "St Pierre et Guines" is illustrated here (no. 0984). Subsequently Calais adopted Bell Punch as their printer; 1d 4625 has obvious Bell Punch serials, and probably dates from the 1890s (32).

(32)

 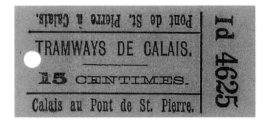

There is not enough time here to examine punch-type tickets from all of the countries which have used them, but it may be of interest to take a look at some early examples, which have a particularly British feel to them. The Tramways Company of Trinidad ticket is helpfully dated (by overprint) 1896 – note that the conditions are almost identical to those on the South London Tramways ticket which we have just examined, and also illustrated are tickets from the Lagos Government Railway tramway, the Camps Bay Tramway Co. Ltd (of Cape Town) and the United Planters Company of Ceylon Ltd (the original operators of the Colombo Electric Tramways) (33)

(33)

  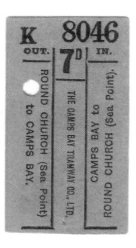

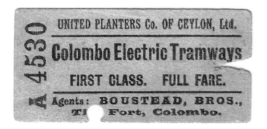

"Geographical" or named-stage punch-types can be fairly attributed to British influence, and some far-flung examples can be seen here. The delightfully-named Rural-Urban Bus Service is from Sierra Leone, while the Bermuda Railway Co. and the Tramways Electricos de Lourenço Marques (of Portuguese East Africa, later if not originally a constituent of Mozambique) are self-explanatory (34).

(34)

After the demise of Whiting in 1906, the Bell Punch company became the undisputed no. 1 printer of punch-type tickets, both in terms of U.K. and overseas customers. As far as the latter were concerned, this prominence continued almost for as long as they continued to produce punch-types; only in Southern Africa, where the not entirely unconnected Lamson Paragon company developed a virtual monopoly, and later in Singapore and Malaysia, did they not control the majority of this business. Williamson had a small share of the overseas punch-type market, notably in Barbados and Mauritius, but the other U.K. printers seem not to have been represented to any great degree. The few examples of others which have come to light include:-

Singapore Electric Tramways Ltd., which in its early days used tickets by J.R. Williams & Co., and subsequently Auto-tickets. (35)

Sierra Leone Railway Bus Services, which used tickets by G.N.P (36)

The Star Ferry (Hong Kong), which was another G.N.P customer in its early days, although I think I am right in saying that tickets were abandoned in favour of turnstiles many years ago. (37)

Pietermaritzburg Corporation (South Africa), which had one set printed by G.N.P

Penang Municipal Bus Service (Malaya), which in the 1950s had sets of tickets by both Punch & Ticket and Oller (as well as several other printers, both U.K and local) (38)

Vacoas Transport of Vacoas, Mauritius, managed to have sets of tickets by Punch & Ticket (although without imprint), Oller and even Auto-Tickets, as well as Bell Punch and Williamson (39).

The Marsamuscetto Steam Ferry of Malta which (like one or two other Maltese undertakings) had tickets printed by Colleys (40).

(35)   (36)   (37)

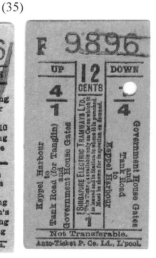

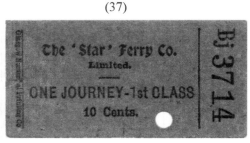

(38)

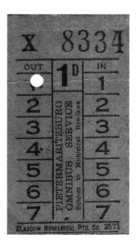

(39)

(40)

In 1913, the majority of the British tramway companies which were members of the B.E.T group adopted a system which was known as "Fair Fare", because it aimed to charge fares which reflected as precisely as possible the distance travelled, with stages in most cases being represented by farthing graduations. The system was cumbersome and proved to be short-lived, but it did produce some very distinctive tickets, of checker-board appearance. Illustrated here are three tickets from different undertakings – a 1¼d. ticket of the Oldham Ashton & Hyde Electric Tramway Ltd, a 3d. of the South Staffs Tramways (Lessee) Co. Ltd, and a 10d. from the Tynemouth and District Electric Traction Co. Ltd. At around the same time, tickets of rather similar appearance were in use in Shanghai; it is tempting to conclude that the "Fair Fare" system was adopted there as well as in the U.K, but I am not entirely convinced that the stages on the Shanghai tickets which I have seen really support this theory. Here are some examples for comparison (41).

(41)

(41 continued)

We will return to punch tickets before we conclude, to look at various oddities, but for now let us move on to some other British ticket exports. The Bellgraphic is well-known in the context of U.K. bus (and some non-transport) operators (42),

(42)

but its use overseas was always limited. However, it was adopted to a degree by a number of African bus operators, in particular members of the "United Transport Group", such as Uganda Transport Co. Ltd, and Nyasaland Transport Co. Ltd.

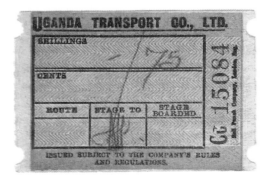
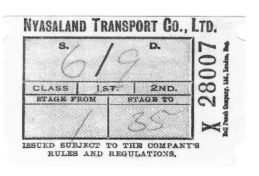

Other African examples include the Rhodesia Touring Co. Ltd, and a single representative from South Africa, namely Kimberley Bus Services (Pty) Ltd, whose tickets bore the imprint "Bell Punch - Lamson Paragon" (43).

(43)

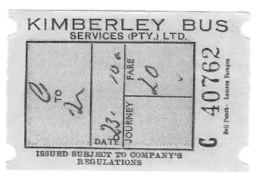

Other examples are known from Ireland (such as Jackson Transport Ltd of Cavan), Jamaica (Mayflower Service for example), and sundry African Railways, where they appear to have been used for conductor-guard issues - a used example from the Gold Coast Railway is illustrated here. One or two Indian issues are also known, such as the East Indian Railway ticket shown here, but I have yet to come across a used example. There was also some limited usage in Australia – perhaps the best known being the Hornibrook Highway Bus Service, which operated services in co-ordination with Queensland Railways' Brisbane suburban trains. An example of their tickets, with fairly elaborate boxes, is illustrated here, together with a rather odd-looking "stock" issue from the 1940s, which according to a note on the back was used on a service from Taree in N.S.W (the operator is unfortunately not mentioned) (44).

(44)

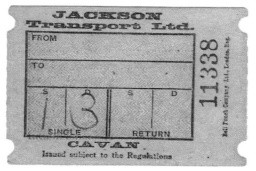
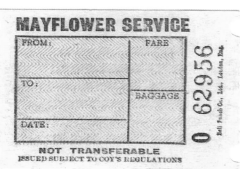

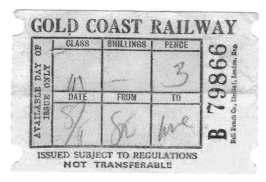
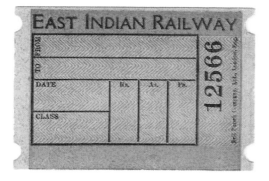

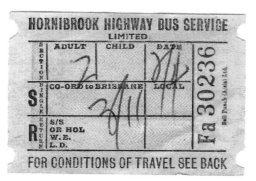
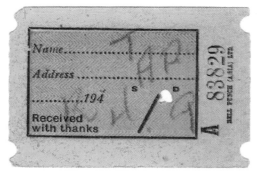

"B.C.C" is Brisbane City Council, and although this early example is in traditional Bell Punch style, it does in fact have the Australasian imprint. Ultimates were also found with several operators in South Africa, but with a couple of late exceptions these were all produced by Lamson Paragon in their own style and format. As noted previously, Lamson Paragon had almost entirely supplanted overseas printers, such as Bell Punch, before the end of the 1920s, and so it is not surprising that they developed their own Ultimate range to meet the needs of the domestic market. Ultimates were also used in a number of European countries at various times, but for the most part these were printed locally, and in formats not necessarily based on anything from the U.K (or anywhere else for that matter).

This leaves us with a few former British territories to examine in terms of "exported" Ultimate tickets. The only examples which come to mind are Ceylon (now of course Sri Lanka) which offers both Colombo Municipal Passenger Transport and the High Level Road Bus Co. Ltd: Jamaica (Bronx Transport for example): Rhodesia (Salisbury United, inter alia), parts of East Africa (again the United Transport connection is the key here - a Nyasaland ticket being illustrated alongside a Salisbury one) and Trinidad (only the memorably - named Sam's Super Services Ltd. is known to me). Two examples are known from Malaya, but these are both believed to have been experimental issues only (45,46).

(45)

(46)

We now turn to a group of ticket types, which whilst of the same family, have varying styles and characteristics. These are known as "talon-valeur" tickets, and their common aspect is that they incorporate one or more sectional divisions, which have to be severed on issue. A key feature is that on issue a section is retained by the issuer (which may be a railway office, or a conductor on a bus, for example), whilst the rest of the ticket is held by the passenger, and that it would be counter-productive to either party if they were to illicitly reduce the portion of the ticket which they hold, as this would either (a) increase the fare to be accounted for, in the case of the issuer or (b) reduce the validity of the ticket, in the case of the passenger.

I know of no reason for the evolution of the respective variants of this concept, but these examples will show that Edmondsons were favoured in Belgium (and hence also the Belgian Congo - examples are also known from Italy), whilst paper tickets of various types are known from Italy (again), Portugal (and Angola), Holland, Germany, Switzerland and South Africa. Note that the Portuguese examples required even more precise cutting than most of the others, because two separate scales are straddled. The Swiss and South African examples are perforated at each section, which seems to add up to a very expensive ticket to produce (47,48,49).

Note that the Portuguese examples required even more precise cutting than most of the others, because two separate scales are straddled. The Swiss and South African examples are perforated at each section, which seems to add up to a very expensive ticket to produce (47,48,49).

(47)

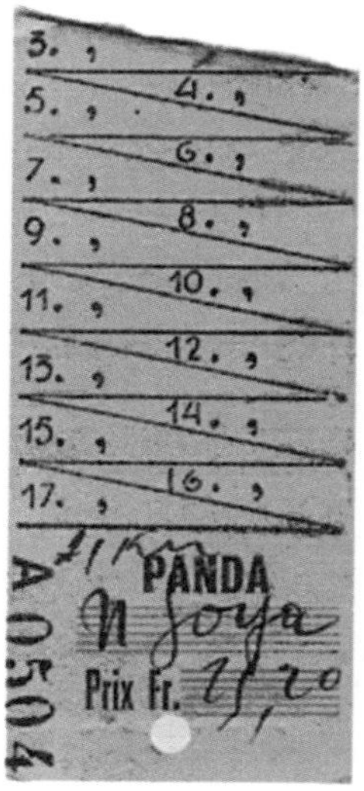

0504
Belgian Congo

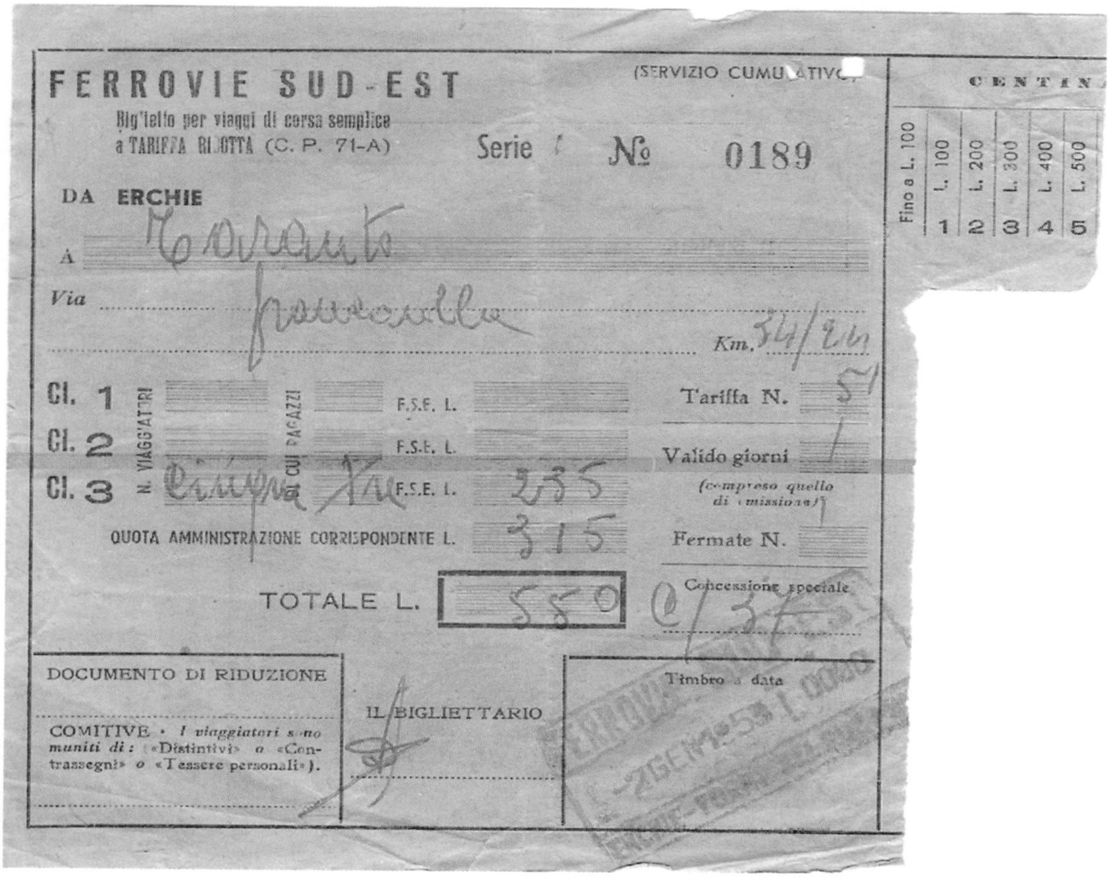

0189
Italy

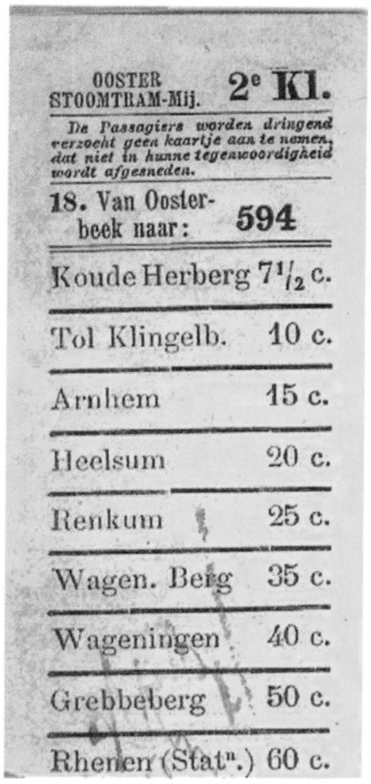

0594
Holland

(48)

80	90 cent.	
70	80 cent.	
60	70 cent.	
50	60 cent.	
40	50 cent.	
30	40 cent.	
20	30 cent.	

1	20 cent.	16
2	Ours | Dailles | Chass.	17
3	A.R.| T | Rosiaz | T |A.R.	18
4	▲ Pt-Ch. ▲ Croix	19
5	St-F. | Lendard	20
6	Sauvab.▼ | Belmt ▼	21
7	— | PL. CENTRALE | —	22
8	▲ Chauderon	23
9	Bois-Vaux	24
10	Chavannes-Crois.	25
11	Dorigny	26
12	Pierrettes	27
13	T | St-Sulp. | T ▼	28
14	Prélaz | Malley TL| Chav. Cr.	29
15	Renges | Pontet | Motty	30
	Chav. Pl. | Poterie | T |Res TL| T	
	B. Site | Scierie | Crissier	
	V. Ste-C. |IIIIIIIIIIII| Mex	31

½	I	II	III	IV	V	VI	R
T	VII	VIII	IX	X	XI	XII	T

AUTOBUS T.L.

Y 26235

26235
Switzerland

13	100	1,10
12	90	1,00
11	80	0,90
9—10	70	0,80
8	60	0,70
7	50	0,60
6	40	0,50
4—5	30	0,40
1—3		0,30

Peenemünde Dorf	Zempin
Peenemünde Nord	Koserow
Karlshagen Dorf	Kölpinsee
Trassenmoor Lager	Ückeritz
Trassenmoor	Schmollensee
Wolgaster Fähre	Seebad Bansin
Bannemin-Mölschow	Seebad Heringsdorf
Trassenheide	Seebad Ahlbeck
Zinnowitz	

Fahrschein gilt auf der durch
Lochung bezeichneten Strecke
Gültig 1 Tag

G № 002263

2. Kl.

Verr.-Bf: Seebad Heringsdorf (A) Personenzug

**Seebad Ahlbeck – Wolgaster Fähre
Zinnowitz – Peenemünde Dorf**

Verr.-Bf: Seebad Heringsdorf (A) Reihe............

Kind

G № 002263

2. Kl.

Personenzug

002263
(East) Germany

B № 11471

6/65-A.D. & CO.-20327-ST/47

GREYHOUND   BUS   LINES

THIS PORTION TO BE RETAINED
BY DRIVER

R1.05 c

95 c

85 c

79 c

74 c

65 c

64 c

59 c

53 c

45 c

43 c

38 c

33 c

30½ c

27 c

THIS TICKET IS NOT TRANSFERABLE
AND IS ISSUED SUBJECT TO THE
REGULATIONS OF THE COMPANY

PASSENGER TO RETAIN THIS
PORTION SHOWING FARE PAID

B № 11471

11471
South Africa

(49)

Bilhete Nº 253785 **B**

I	II	III	IV	V	VI	VII	VIII	IX	X	XI	XII

1	A. Cunhados / A. Francos / Aguas Santas / Alcanede	Carvalhal / Casal do Rei / C. da Marinha / Casalinho		Massuça / Matoeira / Maxial / Miragaia	Sacavém / Salir Matos / Salvador / Sancheira	17
2	ALCOB... / Alcoen... / Ald. Grande	Castanheira / Cátefico / Celo (Ent.)		Moinho Pov / Moita / M. Ferreiros	Sanguinhal / St.ª Caterina / Santa Cruz	18
3	Alenquer / Alfeizerão / Alhandra	Cercal / Chão Rosas / Chegances		M. Redondo / Mosteiros / Murteira	SANTARÉM / Santar. (Est.) / Santa Rita	19
4	Aljubarrota / Alm. Reis / Alto da Serra	Coimbrã / Couto / Cruz Légua		Nadadoura / Nadrupe / NAZARÉ	Santo Antão / São Bartolom / S. Bernardino	20
5	Alverca / Amoreira	Cumeira / Dagorda		Óbidos / Olho Marinho	S. J. Ribeira / São Jorge	21
6	Areia Branca / Assειceira / Ateugsia	Encarnação / Ent. Espanhol / Ereiro		Ota / Outeiro / Palhaça	São Mamede / São Martinho / Sarge	22
7	Aveiras Baixo / Aveiras Cima	Ermegeira / Évora		Patais / Paúl	Securia / Seixal	23
8	Azambuja / Azambujeira / Azcia	Famalicão / Ferrel / Fervença		Penafirme / PENICHE / Peral	S.ª da Luz / Ser. d'El-Rei / Silveira	
9	Baleal / Barosa / Barros	Féteira / Fóz do Arelho / Fráguas		Perna de Pau / Perofilho / Ponte Frielas	Sobral / Tagarro / Tornada	24
10	Barreiros / Bata... / Benedita	Freixeira / Freixofeira / Goeiras (Ent.)		T. VEDRAS / Toxofal / Trabalhias		25
11	Bogalheira / Boiças	Guarita / Guerreiros / Junceira (Ent.)		Ponte Gradil / P. de Loures / Ponte Lousa	Turcifal / Turquel / Valado	26
12	BOMBARRAL / Cabeça Alta / Cadaval	Lameira / Landal / Lepa		Ponte do Rol / Paniével / Porto Lobos	V. S. Quitéria / Vale Cavo / Vale Guarda	27
13	C. RAINHA / Campelos / Caneira	LEIRIA / LISBOA / Loures		P. de St.ª Iria / P. St.ª Adrião / Pavos	Vale Maceira / Valparaiso / Vale da Pinta	28
14	Caniço / Cantarola / Capuchos	Lourinhã / Lousa / Malveira		Pragança / P. Foz Arelho / Quebradas	V. do Pinheiro / V. Raporigas / V. do Velador	29
15	Carrascal / Carresces / Carregado	Manique / Marés / M. Grande		Q.ª Messejana / Q.ª da Seabra / Remalhal	Vermelha / Vidais / V. F. Rosário	30
16	Carreg. (Est.) / Carriche / Cartaxo	Marteleira / M. Joanes / Martingança		Reguengo G. / Reguengo P. / Rib. Crastos / R. Palheiros / R. de S. João / RIO MAIOR	V. F. de Xira / V. N. Rainha / Vilar / Vilgateiro	31

DA CAPISTANO & FERREIRA, L.

ESCUDOS		CENTAVOS	
1			00
2			10
3			20
4			30
5			40
			50

253785
Portugal

6,00	Lobito–Benguela	Ags 7,30 B
5,70	Catumbela–Damba	Ags. 6,00 A
5,30	Lobito–Damba	Ags. 5,70 B
4,80	Lobito–Catumbela	Ags. 5,30 A
3,80	Catumbela–Benguela	Ags. 4,80 B
3,80	Lobito–Benguela	Ags. 3,80 N
3,30	Damba–Benguela	Ags. 3,30 A
3,00	Catumbela–Damba	Ags. 3,20 B
2,80	Lobito–Damba	Ags. 3,00 N
2,50	Lobito–Catumbela	Ags. 2,80 B
1,80	Catumbela–Benguela	Ags. 2,50 N
1,70	Damba–Benguela	Ags. 1,80 B
1,60	Catumbela–Damba	Ags. 1,70 N
0,90	Lobito–Catumbela	Ags. 1,50 N
	Damba–Benguela	Ags. 0,90 N

Caminho de Ferro de Benguela

SIMPLES

VÁLIDO SÓ PARA TRAMUEIS

0987

N.º

1	2	3	4	5	6	7	8	9	10
11	12	13	14	15	16	17	18	19	20
21	22	23	24	25	26	27	28	29	30/31

0987
Angola

022690
Portugal

Companhia Sintra - Atlantico
Sintra-Vila $70

Sintra

2$70 centavos	2$60 centavos	2$40 centavos	2$20 centavos	2$10 centavos	2$00 centavos	1$80 centavos	1$60 centavos	1$50 centavos	1$40 centavos	1$30 centavos	1$20 centavos	1$00 centavos	$80 centavos	$70 centavos	$60 centavos		

				$60	Nunes de Carvalho		
				1$00	$70	Monte Santos	
				1$30	1$00	$80	Ribeira
			2$00	1$60	1$50	1$20	Galamares
			2$80	2$40	2$20	2$00	1$40	Colares
	3$30	3$00	2$80	2$40	1$80	$60	B.ᵃo
3$60	3$30	3$00	2$60	2$00	1$20	$80	Pinhal
4$80	3$70	3$40	3$30	2$70	2$00	1$40	$80	Prais
4$80	4$30	3$90	3$80	3$30	2$60	2$20	1$50	$70
5$00	4$90	4$40	4$20	3$90	3$30	2$70	2$10	1$30	$80	Az.ᵃˢ

Nº 022690

Série B

T. Marias

Incluindo impostos * Conserve-se este bilhete

There was of course also a British invention which displays the features of a "talon-valeur" ticket, but with the added characteristic of a secure repository for the severed parts of issued tickets. I refer to the Willebrew, which was popular with a number of U.K. bus operators from the mid-1930s onwards, but was gradually overtaken by more advanced technology. Most if not all readers will be familiar with the appearance of Willebrew tickets, but here are a handful of uncommon specimens – the L.P.T.B one is the only "geographical" (named stage) example I know of and Kerrs of Methlick, Aberdeenshire was an early and rather surprising user. Willebrews were briefly used by the Ravenglass & Eskdale Railway (although the example here has been punched, rather than "cut"), and also the Falcon Hotel Cliff Lift in Douglas, Isle of Man (50).

(50)

The Willebrew, it is fair to say, did not travel well. I have already suggested that Williamson, who until the very end of the system's life had a monopoly in terms of the printing of the tickets, did not have a vast overseas customer base, and so it is perhaps not surprising that they did not attract very many overseas Willebrew users. Indeed, the only authenticated user is the Sierra Leone Road Transport Corporation, which seems to have had several issues, both wide and narrow, presumably over a period of several years (51).

(51)

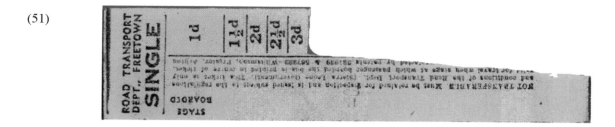

I have used the words "authenticated user" in this context for a reason, namely that I have a number of other Willebrew tickets which are unused specimens, and whose usage in service must be considered doubtful. In this category are Kowloon Omnibus Co. Ltd. (Hong Kong), Kenya Bus Services Ltd., the North West Frontier Province of Rawalpindi, and the Nizam's State Railway of Hyderabad. The Kenya ticket is perhaps the least suspicious, and it is conceivable that they did at least experiment with a Willebrew, but I am hard pressed to imagine their use by the last two operators – the North West Frontier, in particular. My suspicion is that Williamson printed a number of "spoof" issues for distribution at an exhibition of some sort, or alternatively that they sent them to the operators concerned as a marketing tool (52).

(52)

Before leaving "talon-valeur" issues, it is worth mentioning a Scottish variant – which is perhaps stretching the concept of cross-border influence, but nevertheless I will mention it anyway. This is the "Cliptic" system, which involved the use of a special device combining a punch and a cutter – a Willebrew with a difference, perhaps. I think I am right in saying that this was produced and marketed by Glasgow Numerical Printing, but it clearly did not sell well, and the only substantive user known is Dunoon Motor Services Ltd; neighbouring Gold Line was also a user in a limited way, and may have taken over one or two of Dunoon Motor Service's "Cliptic" cutters. Such tickets as have been seen from Gold Line do not, incidentally, appear to have been printed by G.N.P. Similar tickets were also used by the Invergarry and Glenquoich Mail Service, but all those which I have seen have been punched (in other words as a multi-value ticket), and I do not know if they ever used, or even took delivery of, a "Cliptic" (53).

(53)

We now need to consider some other examples of cross-border influence from non-U.K. sources. North America (U.S and Canada) has always adopted its own systems and practices in preference to imported ones, but by the same token has not in general had a major influence elsewhere. However there are a few rather surprising examples which we can address here.

Firstly, we have the Tranvias Electricos de Caracas (Caracas Electric Tramways) of Venezuela, which used very obviously American tickets, printed by Globe. There is nothing very odd about this, but there are also very similar examples which were printed by G.N.P – and this is extremely strange, particularly as (a) G.N.P as previously noted are not renowned for the size of their overseas clientele (b) this type of ticket clearly does not come from their standard portfolio (54).

(54)

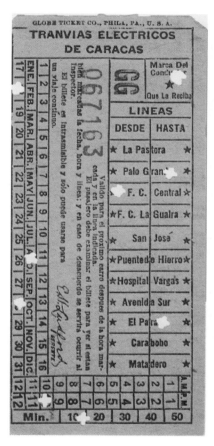
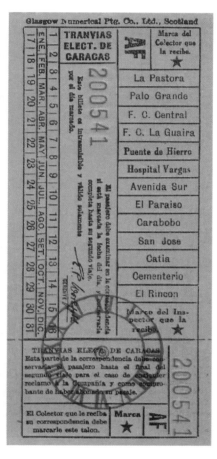

American influence has also been noted in several Caribbean islands, even those former British territories which might have been expected to have been Bell Punch customers first and foremost. To an extent, they did indeed adopt British systems – but both Barbados and Trinidad seem to have dabbled with American-style tickets as well. I am not entirely sure where the West Indian Electric Company hails from, but Trinidad seems most likely. Note also the Bell Punch printed punch-type from the Arima Bus Service Association (again from Trinidad), which is in a very unusual format; the inclusion of two facsimile signatures again suggests American influence (55).

(55)

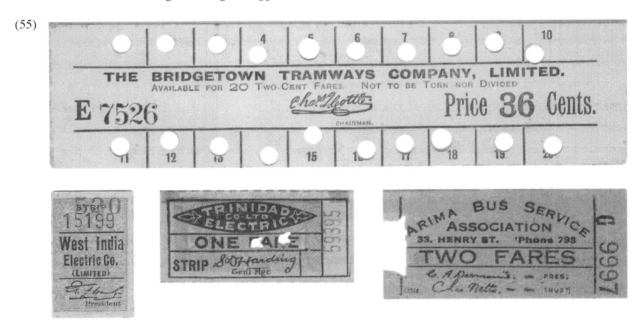

We should not overlook the rather odd Weekly Passes which were used between 1924 and 1940 by Bradford, Doncaster and Hull municipalities, and which show Copyright Design No. 251923. The design of these has a distinctly American flavour, but the background to their origin and usage remains something of a mystery. Here are examples from both Doncaster and Hull (56).

(56)

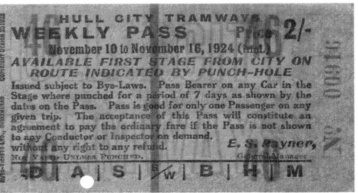

Moving on from America, there are some examples of German-printed tickets from territories where they might not be expected. In Egypt, for example, both Cairo and Alexandria used very typical German paper tickets, printed by Fassbinder of Berlin, before the Second World War. Here are examples of both, plus in the case of Alexandria an almost equally surprising one printed in Italy by Massarani of Torino (Turin) (57).

(57)

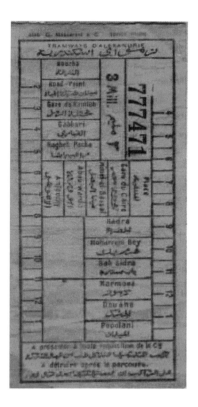

More recently, there were some interesting examples of German-printed tickets in West Africa. I happened to stumble on the story behind these when I visited Ghana in 1977, and this can be summarised as follows. In the course of an attempt (which met with limited success) to secure some withdrawn tickets from the Omnibus Services Authority in Accra, I was introduced to a couple of German consultants, who were advising the Authority on a number of strategic issues, including fares and fare collection. They had recently undertaken a similar assignment in Freetown, Sierra Leone, where they had been commissioned to investigate the massive shortfall between actual and expected takings from fares.

The Germans did not take long to discover the reason for this shortfall. At the time of their arrival, the Road Transport Corporation had been using T.I.Ms, and the conductors had mastered the inner workings of the machines to the extent that they could effectively decide how much of the takings they wished to hand over to the Corporation, and how much they preferred to keep for themselves. The consultants immediately withdrew the machines, and substituted pre-printed and serially-numbered paper tickets; reflecting their connections these were printed in Germany by Schwarz of Miesbach. There were two sets – a very plain one for local services, and a delightful set in classic German "netzbild" style, showing the network of country services in diagrammatic form. In the event I did not manage to obtain any examples of these until I myself visited Sierra Leone in 1984, by which time tickets were still in the same format, but printed locally. Incidentally, the one used "netzbild" example which I found then reflected an extension to the earlier network, to include cross-border services to Conakry (Guinea) and Monrovia (Liberia).

But returning to Ghana, the situation as regards fare collection was rather different, because there were no machines to give offence, and indeed in 1977 the Omnibus Services Authority were using punch-types, some of them being Bell Punch (Hong Kong) prints. Nevertheless, as I only found out many years later, the consultants had imposed German tickets on Accra, albeit in a much smaller format. The printers were again Schwarz of Miesbach (58).

(58)

 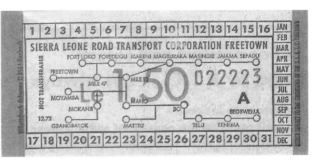

A part of the world which has for a number of years produced punch-type tickets of consistently high quality is of course South-East Asia, and specifically Malaysia and Singapore. It would have given me great pleasure to be able to illustrate a ticket from one of my favourite printers, Phoenix Press of Penang, for a bus company in Africa, the Caribbean or even the U.K. Sadly I cannot do so, as to the best of my knowledge Phoenix only ever printed for operators in peninsular Malaysia. However, a slightly earlier printer, Bus & Theatre Tickets Ltd. of Singapore, did at least produce some very respectable punch-types for a handful of operators in Malaysia, both on the peninsula, and across the South China Sea in Sarawak. (Sarawak has always had a rather mixed approach to tickets, with a number of operators having favoured punch-types, whilst others used paper tickets; British North Borneo, further up the coast, however, never seems to have taken to punch-types at all, at least as far as bus issues are concerned). Here are a couple of examples of Bus & Theatre Tickets' products: The City Transport Service of Penang, again, and the Sungei Merah Bus Service of Sibu, Sarawak (both front and back of the latter ticket are illustrated, as it will be seen that the front is untitled) (59).

(59)

  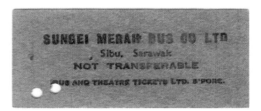

I would like to conclude by taking a look at a few examples of punch-type tickets from rather surprising users; and then to consider where one might have expected to find them but in practice they are either very few and far between, or they are non-existent.

First, then, the surprises. I have already highlighted a couple of Calais punch-types, which are not what one might have expected, but perhaps at the time when they were produced alternative systems were less readily available. Also early, certainly pre-1900, are some rather striking tickets from certain Dutch steam-tram operators (60). They claim to be "Bell Punch" issues, and indeed this description appears in English on some of the tickets; also they have certain characteristics of punch-types, in particular the background repeats in the punching areas, but I would suggest that they are not true punch-types as we would normally describe them.

(60)

On the other hand, the next three tickets (61) are very clearly the genuine article, and two of them are clearly Bell Punch company productions. The latter are from Sweden and Belgium, the exception is the W & B Electricity Co. Ltd. issue from Italy.

(61)

 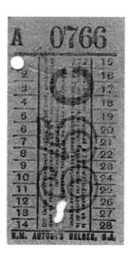

Some other rather unlikely issuers would include Salem Ali Abdoo of Aden, the Khuzistan Bus Service of Abadan, Persia (now Iran), and the Canal Army Bus Service (62).

(62)

So, what of the ones which have slipped the net, or have very nearly done so? The most obvious area which has largely eschewed punch-types, despite long-standing U.K. ties, is Australasia. It is not quite true to say that punch-types are unknown in Australia, but the only example I have come across which was printed in England is an early Bell Punch issue from Hobart Municipal Tramways; unfortunately this has suffered a little from water at some stage in its long life. Bell Punch (Australasia) clearly had the capacity to print punch-types, and a uniquely Australian untitled, or "stock" ticket type has been seen; exactly how widespread this was is not known, but it was certainly used for a while by Blue & White of Sandgate, near Brisbane. The same operator is also known to have had a more modern style of punch-types subsequently. Early Brisbane Tramways tickets could arguably be described as punch-types, but in my view this is questionable (63).

(63)

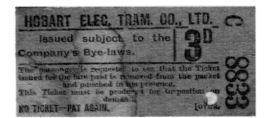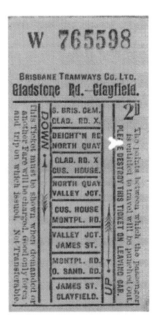

Moving across to New Zealand, which one might expect to have been a keen user of punch-types, I have not been able to discover a single one; on the contrary, New Zealand seems to have adopted a very individual approach to ticket practice from a very early stage.

One final example is British North Borneo, which is now the Malaysian state of Sabah. We have seen that there were at least some punch-types used in neighbouring Sarawak, but the bus operators in North Borneo are not known to have used anything other than paper pad tickets. Curiously, however, the railway did have punch-types of a sort – here is an early example with British North Borneo State Railway title (64),

(64)

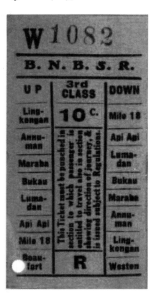

together with a couple of later issues, illustrating the sequence of subsequent titles (65).

(65)

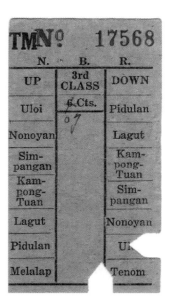

In conclusion I hope that this address will have stimulated further thought and discussion. In the course of preparing it, I have been delighted to discover new angles and connections as I have been through my collection – in some cases these might not have come to light otherwise – and I am sure that there are others. I shall be only too pleased to receive comments, and additional contributions to the subject.

John King
January 2009